Creature

Pitt Poetry Series

Terrance Hayes
Nancy Krygowski
Jeffrey McDaniel

Editors

Creature

Marsha de la O

University of Pittsburgh Press

Published by the University of Pittsburgh Press, Pittsburgh, Pa., 15260
Manufactured in the United States of America
Printed on acid-free paper
10 9 8 7 6 5 4 3 2 1

ISBN 13: 978-0-8229-6723-1
ISBN 10: 0-8229-6723-5

Cover art: L. I. Henley, *Heart & Thread*. Courtesy of the artist.
Cover design: Melissa Dias-Mandoly

Toda la luz del mundo cabe dentro de un ojo.

—Federico Garcia Lorca

Contents

III

IV

V

Creature

I

To Be Unprotected

Alone, under a blue cloud backlit
by a quarter moon in a dry wash,
I wanted starlight to bend low
brush my face and bare arms.
There's a thirst inside syntax
for what can't be told: night breaking
against a bowl of mountains, heart
ticking each unit of flux.
When I say I heard it, I mean
I felt its song on my skin in needles
in shards raining like flakes
from a hammerstone.
Feathered, rippled, stroke-struck.
Inside my body, a hum or tremble
in a place where I keep fear,
outside, a glister, a lilt, falling
as sound from stars
like tin, like salt, like silt. Words
can't mean the same thing twice.
When I say I thought I might die
of beauty, I mean it broke me apart.
I had to give in, let night drape
a garment of sound over my human
form. Let words yearn toward
silence, under the piano of starlight.
Its soft percussion.
If wild is psalm and singer, let
it wash over, empty me, and
make use of my emptiness,
I am willing.

My father died in the fullness of spring

as petals began to brown. New buds were forming, but not many.
Was it glorious? It was.
Our backyard, like an aging showgirl.

He nourished himself with light like any other plant.
He would raise his chin and close his eyes.

He sang snatches of Bing Crosby ballads, could whistle
on-key. He did not admit that he loved me.

I never saw him cry until very late. He could keep it soundless.
Control his breath. Be silent,

                        as a tear rolled down his cheek.
Then another, and another.

In this drought, I save every drop for my flowers. Some last only a day.

He didn't acknowledge weakness. Or complain.
But, over years, would not tend himself,

body and mind, a forgotten garden.

Horses Resting

The horses gather beneath the oak, maybe curious
    about the wagon and the man, or his horse. They sense
still-tender green shoots in the mottled shade

But don't stretch their long necks down, now that quiet
    has taken them, held in each other's presence,
their bodies close in shadow.

Sunlight collects in pools on the open road, yet in shade
    falls like bits of mosaic glass, the smell of heat and dust
and light-seared grass, scent of the world wanting its water
    on this parched earth.

They look to be bays in the photo, though the far one,
    a chestnut, has turned to nuzzle the flank of the gray
gelding in harness between cart shafts. The gray
    gently rolls the snaffle bit in his tender mouth.

The shared being of herd animals ripens into quietude
    that even the driver leaning against the tree can feel—
horses drowsing together, as if drowsing were wisdom
    or fullness, and he wonders

How it is that being among beasts of burden could feel like
sharing company with languid angels. And thinks that
    such closeness is also spacious, and their quiet involves
the silence of the oak and its gracious shadow, as though

Peace were part of the water table at the roots of the tree.

What It Sounded Like on The Way to Calvary

Sparrows bathing in puddles

As the sun passes behind a cloud

The scrape when the wheel heaves

On its wooden pin

Slough brimming

Gold roof of water, plash of bare feet

Her blue shift hitched up

Baby sister milking their mother, jaw pulsing

These small things changed her

Meat-birds on the scaffold

A woman turning her back

A woman sobbing into her apron

Brick-red earth

Trail of One Hundred Giants

Whitethorn, in heat-struck flower—
as for the grove, it stands
                    like scaffolding under the city of heaven
          some men still imagine.

Loneliness does not destroy the possibility of loneliness.

And the mind this past year has moved
                                        to another place
where what was once strength and withstood,
                                        became suddenly fragile.
As if the soul were being forced to choose
in the presence of a demon explaining that yes, you have to
do it all again in exactly the same way.

Now the wind in the sequoias
          plays its infinite cantata, now many tongues
in the small bells of the largest lives
                              roll and resound;
their sound an invisible river.

Suppose god exists, and they are wind
                              in consort with evergreens.
The sighing body, singing body. Roar and
hush, motion and stillness that enters the breastbone.

The giants declare their holiness
by living. Their roots spread ever outward.

I passed miles through blackened remains
                    of the southern Sierras to stand here.

They're searching for water.

Gods in Ruins

Today, a crow stopped me. Something invisible
          wound around her neck. Fishline?

Feathers effaced and raw skin flagrant. No perch,
          she's on the concrete dipping her head

toward puddle water in the gutter. Throat
          yoked tight, as though wearing a necklace

of red beads. Just at the edge of motion and
          stillness. And now this thirst,

this desire for a last sip of water. If she
          can dip her beak, bring it up,

tilt her head back at the right angle. And
          she manages. Slowly. As though

she understands her life has run out.
          How not to think of Emerson,

how not to think of the way he spoke
          of man, of *us*, as 'gods in ruins,' and

his emphasis was 'gods' but, oh, the ruins—
          if he could see all we've brought down.

The Hidden World

A youth walks toward where I stand
beside a white Impala, its backseat full
of flowers, a cavern filled with scent.
I recognize him; he sees who I am.
I can say this happened in alluvial
night, in night as dark as the pupil
of my eye, as extinct stars.
I can say that night still exists,
it's ongoing, it's a basin of indigo
water. We are waist-deep
in what seems all past and present
now that death is your home, you,
the boy who once lived, as old
as you will ever be.
I see your face again. Your lanky
grace. And happiness distills me
to a word—your name, Sanchez.
That I could know so fully
what it is to cherish. Know
how tenderness pours itself on grief.
Where there should only be nothing,
something moves; some power
has divulged itself at last. And, if not,
where came these thousand blossoms?

A History of Lament

You would never think so, but the detail is movement.
Not his body, blue beneath the skin, a severed rope
around his waist, the other one fled beyond the high
pure cry of geese over Mt. Ararat with its dirty shawl of snow.

Yes, I have a litany. I can't breathe. I have to go on. Sorrow
does not end. Once, I was the first of my kind, the first lover
of flowering plants, the water lily, lotus, magnolia.
Not anymore. My solution is the mountain itself, hard

on the outside, hot liquid held at the center. Now I am granite,
flint, myself the mortar and fiery pestle, rocky plates
scraping themselves away. I wear adamant like a cloak.

The one sun that remains sheds his light over crags
and blocks of stone. And a seed splits open in the cleft.
What will become a tree—slowly grows.

Crevasse

I no longer believe in Tierra del Fuego.
We'll probably never arrive. Already I'm gray

as granite, and know well how to lower my head,
how to lock my tongue with my teeth. I will need

four legs and sharp hooves now. I will need
a long strong spine and the ability to trudge.

The snow falls thick and will cover my fetlocks
but how else can I carry all your provisions

over the Hindu Kush? A crevasse is a crack
as deep as woe. To divide the genders, we use

a slash. And if late in your wanderings you come
to my barrow, ask yourself, is she in there, does

she wait for me? Yes, yes, I am no longer a beast.
Roll away the boulder blocking the doorway.

You may hear small shrieks, difficult to decode:
God hasn't given us the punctuation.

I'll be wrapped in a cloak of needles, but look closely,
I beg you. In my want, I resemble any other ghost.

Portrait of my Father, Mise en Scène

I don't see him, he's nowhere. He's already set me
on a stool at his work table to help,

filling one-ounce bottles of acetone and lacquer thinner
from a spigot attached to a five gallon can,

the liquid clear with poison vapor or faintly gold and viscous.

The bottles march one by one to the spigot,
my sticky amber soldiers wheeling abreast, each

little man stepping up. The fluid fills them.

Dusty skylight above this table large enough
for all the pieces. Glass from Germany. From Belgium.

From Italy. The rondelles, the colored glass, milk glass,
painted glass, stained glass. Nothing is clean.

Shattered roses, violets torn from their vines,
I'm alone. He's somewhere out back, he's gone.

The ex-cons work the loading dock. Picking and packing.
Stacking boxes on pallets. Grief has kept them lean.

Light banks against their work desks, the kind of light
that pools when you're going through the motions, when

you can't live in the body you're in, but you can make it move.

I've been warned not to speak to any of them.
Not to let my eyes meet theirs.

They do not hurry; they bend over their work
as if they could fold the past just so,

and fit it into a box sealed with strapping tape.
As if exile were reverie.

Without meeting their eyes, I breathe in their atoms, I breathe
in the heat shimmering off the nape of their necks

from the small flame, always lit, of bitterness,
which is also called coming-to-work,

also bereavement.

The grainy light through the dust and chicken-wire
pours over my shoulders, over the fissure

separating mother from child, shepherd from sheep,
Christ from the pain he crouches beneath—

all ministered to on my father's grimy table.

II

The Seer and the Seen

All things therefore are charged with love . . . and
if we know how to touch them, give off sparks
and take fire.
            —Gerard Manley Hopkins

If fish could swim into air and feed on brilliance—
that light-thrashed frenzy, that glory-cloud of jots and zags:
gold dragonflies with golden wings.

And he in their midst
                    almost as if they'd called him.
Almost as if to say,
                    Here, stranger, you can safe-keep your love, here.
Say it was like that…

            ———

The stars are like letters
                    that inscribe themselves every moment,
whispers Plotinus. Across centuries.
                            And didn't the diminutive
Jesuit seek to descry them,

didn't he translate as best he could? He came
to his writing desk
                    which was failure
whenever he could bear it.

            ———

If Plotinus was right, then he is right:
Desire is seated in the soul,
                    and iridescence dwells
in the retina.

If *it is not possible to distinguish*
                    between the seer and the seen,

then god must be present
both in the world and our gaze.

Attention's lifted and carried,
a man gathered into the visible so utterly,
                                        landscape unladens itself,
love loosens,
            that's it: the new word is *inscape*.

————

The cornea is nourished by tears.
At the moment of greatest intensity, comes
            the next moment:
the cant of the seen world, the warp, the question of lack.

Father Flaw. Father Daft. Separation.
He died in a crumbling stone house in Dublin, his city of exile,
believing his poems would never be seen.

Near the end, he insisted something terrible had happened
            to his eyes.
The old stories said dragonflies, like us,
                                        are capable of harm:
eye-pokers, darning needles: they'll sew your lids shut.

————

On that last walk out, he imposed
                        on himself
'the discipline of the eyes,'
his penance looking down, his refusal,

but he could not choose not to feel the gaze
            from the emissary,
green bound in its body,
                        tendril twine-twirled,
to raise his face, be held in the stem,
            the life-rush between them,

to behold leaf-light
        like a headwind off ecstasy,
                like a drift of ether,
   like a loose halo.

After some time, returned
       to where pain kept him.

———

Say it's mostly about loss then…
        Except maybe he disappeared into joy
in those weeks of fever, a thorn flicking loose
          in the cornea
and ripping sideways, the sheath torn—

as vision filmed over, dragonflies swarmed;
         as light snows,
as they blizzard air with gold,
         oh, star shapes:
    to take in fully
that fire changes everything,
       how lucent the flames
   where love burns.

Creature

It's mild November, smoke blown out
to sea, fires waning. I'm in the kitchen
looking up from time to time and out
the living room window to the olive tree.
On the other side, hummingbirds zoom
and pause, a midair blur of motion
and stillness, sipping the last few blossoms
on the lanky butterfly bush, long curved
sword flowers gone black and crumpled
before they fall. A small insistent wind
flows through the partly open window.
The world can enter, I'm not trapped
in here. An open window, and the sense
that more than air is coming through,
more than air and light, more than wind,
still gentle, but with a little beveled edge.
Remembering itself to me. Fires smolder
ten miles away. The glass is flawed. All
is quiet change. Flecked patterns of
moving shadow. The rise and fall of wind.
Vagaries of dust. All is quiet. The sun is
doing what it has done from the beginning.

All transfigures in an instant. A flailing noise,
glass shaking in its frame, what could it be,
this sound, so lost and angry, so alive?
And there she is, a hawk in my alien
living room battering her wings against
the baffling solidity of air, a hawk trapped
in a paroxysm of fear, led astray into the
human, our box-like rooms, our prisons,
bewilderment cloaking both our minds.
And here we are, the bird and I,
in different and staggering worlds
where transparencies are impassable.
How many times have I sensed myself
as though behind glass, my isolation

excluding others, and always,
it seemed, the real world just beyond?
Getting out is a matter of life and death.
As though I could kill her by looking at her,
so much more frantic she grows as I creep
toward the window, my eyes on her talons,
her terrible beak. She rises higher above
the couch toward the low ceiling, her wings
still thrashing against the glass, the world
she came from right there in front of her.
I see what she is, a Cooper's hawk, a juvenile,
her golden head and streaky breast. She made
a mistake and hurtled through the air into loss.
Now the only thing to do is drop my gaze,
head down, pull the window fully open, throw
open the door, the double doors in the dining room,
rush to the garage to remove my hateful presence.

When I said, Doctor, I'm the one I'm trying
to set free, she nodded as though in approval,
and I felt at once how craven my need
for approval, but still I went on, I'm willing
to do the work, but don't ask me to pray—
those words with their contained half-smile,
and again she nodded—*was* she approving?
Then she asked, Have you ever felt an energy,
perhaps even a feminine energy? I shook
my head. But standing, shaking in the garage,
it must be a god I'm praying aloud to—the life force
itself whose name is creature—saying, creature,
you can do it, you can find your way, creature.

Omens

1.

They said it started with a man who lit
a campfire on a warm night in autumn.
In what we called autumn, though summer
never really ended but the winds came.

The rainy season began, but no rain fell.
Did he think the winds were bringing
cooler air and kneel down to light his fire,
this stranger they identified as the source?

The officials never talk about him now.
Maybe he never existed. The stranger. The mistake.
The campfire. After what happened, it's only human
to ascribe blame. To let it fall on a stranger.

The arroyo is green again, rains came down
in spring. Our earth is warming. That fire
waited years, biding its time, waiting on the future
while chaparral oozed oil, and heat notched up.

There were two pine trees
growing in the arroyo,
their roots deep in what moisture
could be found.

2.

The hills went up like tinder
because they were tinder and spread the flames
everywhere, yet the fire followed
the path of water, the hottest burns

in the arroyos that briefly fill with rain,
those small dry brooks that live awhile
beneath the silt and nourish the above-world.
The two pine trees grew just there.

One of them held a bulky nest made of sticks:
a house that crows built. They chose a pine,
and not an oak. I often stopped for a bit
to watch them raise their young.

They'd double-clutched, caring for a full nest
into fall. The father sometimes perched in an oak
and conversed with the mother across the canyon
as she tended their nestlings.

What weight the future levies on the present.
But crows seem equal to it. We like to think they are
what we're not: that wild means capable.
The fire knew the path and fell upon the pines.

3.

I didn't return for a long time.
It was forbidden for months
and when finally allowed,
still I hesitated.

Both pines were dead.
One remains standing, completely blackened,
a skeleton, no life hidden in the wood.
Death in the shape of a tree.

The other pine, the one that cradled the nest,
is utterly gone, no sign that it ever stood.
A little grass grows at the base and there's a space
in air where all that happened is annulled.

Strange that the tree of death consoles me
and the tree that disappeared confounds me—
that bare place where only emptiness remains.
I'm astonished by absence; it's an absolute.

4.

They must have been fledglings, big enough
to fly, and flown to safety.
We can't know who will be spared,
or what will happen to the earth.

I still see the adults, they haunt the burnt arroyo
that soon as ever grew a blanket of flowers,
mustard and wild carrot. I can hardly look
at the blooms. All that life, the weight of

the future, flammable tinder. Most of the oaks
survived. They don't set down roots
in a watercourse, somehow, they know better.
The oaks are scorched, but not so bad they can't go on.

That's where I saw the pair of crows,
the male high in what's left of the crown,
the female down below in shadow.
The male calling in hoarse, eager tones; the female silent.

The Afterlife of Flames

After fire blackens the earth,

after a scarf of smoke presses

against the wound, the embryo

inside its sack, ripe and resting

in a chemical sleep, there's

no need to abide any longer,

no need for the abode, the

hut, the hull, the home, only

translation is required to un-

coil a long-limbed seed, a pip

braiding itself into a child

the color of sunset, four petals,

naked stem, one bloom arching

its narrow body over harm.

In This Time of Parched Things

I speak out loud to a lizard. I say, "you have *such* a short tail,"
he doesn't respond, so I add, "you hold it up beautifully."

He comes closer. He's a miniature wild burro in tall grass
and a moment later, extending his neck, a bird dog
gathering scent. The arch in his back is gorgeous.

In August, they're like this, lithe and muscular.

Lifting his tail, he streaks along the stone wall. I watch—
it's almost kinship I feel. Have I become his little mother?

Once I had a son. He was lost on Day of the Dead
in the parking lot in front of Walmart. Where the wind twitches.

I wanted to name him for the boy next door who never came back.
I wanted to grow him a heavy brow and magical feet, flesh
of ash and glint.

Now, my lizard gathers himself in full sun to harvest light. His black
eye meet my gray. One teaspoon of alligator, a spoonful
of philosopher, a mouthful of daggers.

His tessellated armor conceals a private, tender blue. Raptor boy.
Serpent boy.

Once, I asked for a different body.

American Megafauna

Our father leaking blood and water, our
father leaking earth.

A private in the army back-when,
enjoying free food and small duty until

they meant to send him to Korea
if he didn't shape up: he rose to corporal,

his first child was born. He got a second job
from late afternoon on. Oklahoma.

Where light lasts so long you can work two jobs
and get home by full dark.

The venerable American mastodon—
our incognitum, our ritual for vanishing.

As we are his witnesses. As his blood chutters
in our veins. As he is arterial. As he is my artery.

Chutter: an alarm call by vervets in the presence
of a snake; to make such a call, to cry danger.

The shudder in my body as I knock
in the morning. Everywhere the holy spirit and fear.

It's late and he hasn't come out. Light: full.
Body: stretched out. As blood throbs. I hear him—

he's alive—he's saying It's a beautiful spring morning,
he's saying what time is it, he's saying I can get up.

The dig at El Fin del Mundo exposes
elephant bones scattered near spearpoints.

The trapped animal no longer trumpets.
He rears up, lunges forward as blood smarts.

All our fathers, titans of the Ice Age,
great beasts, their sparse ginger hair,

their black gone silver, once ensnared
they linger on the surface for months.

When I say holy spirit I mean
that which is elusive and everywhere.

That which we all share.
Water is holy to shark. Fire to lodgepole.

Soft air over the seep lacquered with leaves
to my incognitum, my
                    father, sinking.

III

The Day I Was Protected

I am the harsh sound a tool makes, a small cutting wheel scoring a surface, scribing a line. Briefly, intense heat is generated, briefly, the glass cries out, a hurting sound; they wound each other in their touching: steel and annealed glass.

The glazier is angry but careful, he taps along the line he's made and breaks the glass with his hands, moving quickly, he doesn't wear gloves. He picks up the cutter to score the next piece.

Have you ever felt a hive mind, a swarm in light that falls slant, a presence? The glazier is my father.

In those days, stained glass comes from Europe in boxes in the hulls of freighters.

I am eight years old at this time. My father is making a lantern for my mother, but he stops when the man comes in.

I use a boxcutter to slit the seams, rondelles from Belgium stacked inside, lift out honey-colored disks and hold them up to high windows. The column of my arm, my candelabra fingers.

My father lets me play with glass, with lead, with boxcutters. I never touch the soldering iron.

He's angry at the man who came in from the loading dock. A small, thick man in a sports jacket.

Did you know dragonflies see more light than us? Their eyes absorb colors beyond our range. And they catch the image faster (a ripple in the amplitude of air). Their brains evolved to process light.

Blood thrumming, drum-heart knocking, throat clenched. The harsh sound of breath shuttles through my narrow passage. The man is talking to my father.

First, he makes a purchase, the lantern my father made for my mother; my father sold my mother's gift. Then the man asks, how much for the little girl? My father laughs and says she's not for sale. The man begins to bid, he offers a price, then a higher one. Not for sale, says my father. Another offer, and another. Outside, cars are stopped on Western Avenue, waiting for the light to change.

I look over at my father transfigured, his eyes opaque, his milk-glass eyes that do not see, his metallic hands, fists tight, holding the cutter, bearing down on an ache of glass. Snick of the wheel, sharp hone of steel, abrupt crack, white sound of breaking shoots across the sheet. He's ripping glass in two over and over, glass is shrieking under his weight. The glass howls, the glass screams. He keeps working, head down. There are no words.

That was the day I was protected. The man paid $50 for the lantern and offered $100 for the child. I knew that day my father cared for me more than he needed money, and we did need money. I knew that day I had a home, the walls were made of glass, there was a horizon beyond.

Indelible

Telling your story after 36 years means you've been
carrying a bag of silence laced all over with veins
the whole time, it's you, your blood pumping
through what happened, a second bladder with
a blue shine and finally an opening, it's a panic
closet expanding to compass a continent,
an entire landmass of aging women waiting to spill,
afraid to spill. It's incontinence. Their laughter's
thunder, it means they'll attack you, track you
down and stand under your window. Your sister's
still gonna cry and her tears will run down
her furrows. The needle's at zero—they'll say
you're a liar—but keep talking: you've been
zero since you were twelve or nine or fifteen.

※

As if you could bring the words out
on a lead rope and lunge them
in the arena, as if they're nickering
in the straw waiting their turn,
as if the words wanted that:
to be trained or tamed, as if
they could help doing harm.

※

Once I stepped through a door
in the air and the house didn't exist.

※

Question: What has to happen? Question: Why?

※

Oh, don't ask why. Girls die
every day for no reason.
                    You have a few seconds.
There's concrete, and a race a girl might win.

And you do. And two weeks later,
you open the Herald Examiner.
The girl who died in your place
is Vietnamese, there's her photo:
anyone could see what just
happened—one small hand
fumbling to button her top,
the other helping her auntie up,
exactly as the soldiers say.
The journalist snapped the shot
and she flew into the ether to die
on and on around the world.

※

They say for the dead to fly
the wick of pure loneliness
must stay lit.
Or ghosts plunge from the sky.

※

Now love can never unwrap her long black hair.

※

If we planted a tree for every
dead girl, we'd live in a forest.

※

I carry my fear, it's portable,
the better to wander
among a scattered congregation
of trees.
From where I stand,
this might be a forest,
unseen birds and seen.
A mockingbird held at a distance
of forty yards by a guard jay.
The shiver in wind
of the variegated branch,
first fuchsia in March
the color of shrimp.
Each tree an absence.

Let's go to the forest and wander
like Aeneas wandering through hell
holding a bough to stay safe.
Let's go to the forest where trees are prisms,
archives of light, they hold the body.

Because I would not accept his
advances, I was sealed in a tree.
At first, between my body
and the bark, a narrow space,
like I'd once imagined the gap
between desire and fate. I knew
better than to struggle. It's not
a lie to say my heart drummed
in my throat. *Change my
form, release my sorrow.*
I'd petitioned the fathers.
Sensation of toes spread

and digging in. And then they
didn't exist. Legs knobbed
into wood, a hard sheath over
my trunk, my crown. But I
could still feel the strong blue
stare of light. And a secondary
light of understanding. Now
that god could not hurt me,
the world was out there,
like a book, something
I could learn to read.

Origin

Say a cloud carries storm,
cups fire.

The dark coil swims upward,
the gyre swarms down.

The baby weighs
six pounds

and is swaddled in flames.
The baby sears

everyone's eyes.
Say my mother is a chalice

for wind, say she's a boat
made of snow.

There's a face inside
her face that fits

exactly over
my skull:

a white room
with five locked doors

where I love her
like a magpie, a savage.

Say she disappears
when light leaps,

a lit panther at the edge
of the world, my

volatile crystal,
my bell of the storm.

Afterward

They called me Eastside at school.
Afterward, no safe corners left.
My stuffed animals never blinked.

Did you know the third little pig
survived hidden in a churn? A tree
can grow through your face; it makes

a perfect mask. You stop up your ears
by buzzing in the back of the throat.
How the forest masses on the north-

facing slope. I fly there to listen to
the wind. To watch words riffle
as leaves turn in what they call

the book of life. I should say some-
thing about how to go on: you have
to press yourself into a churn. Become

misshapen. The child is mother
to the woman. Just as a seed grows
into a tree, a wooden child carves

herself in slats. And wood has a long
memory. My mother calls it shame.
But I've learned other words.

The Boy Who Went Looking

I was espiritu santo, piñon fire–those flames.

I ran the raggedy edge of downslope winds,

turned into a marsh hawk over Cuyama.

I was a little girl under Zaca Lake. I was

opaque. Given petals floating on the surface,

I swallowed. I was quartzite, abalone shell.

Every day I searched for my mother.

I was hidden in a white man's pocket.

At the river, I became a pole bridge,

a rope, I was hand-over-hand. Once

I saw a ball of light moving slowly down

the track. I ran, but could not reach her.

Now, I wait. I wait. When people ask,

I don't answer. Silence is also speech.

Girls in Custody

Let's start here: her neck bent at an odd angle,
        the light stippled, the door closed.

Later they would explain she had made it difficult to see
        into her room, they were in a meeting.

She's alone in the heavy air thinking of Trayvon Martin, how she got
        to Juvenile Hall after she went to a rally for Trayvon

and didn't ask her probation officer. Thinking of skittles in rainbow
    colors,
        and how black the night when you might not make it home.

Adults here don't know anything about crime.
        She could tell them if she could tell them.

She's thinking of that word "remanded," of "defying authority," "public
        intoxication." She is thinking of the idea of home.

Above her, the light is a white rush.
        And now she'll be a little part of that rush.

She wishes an old wish: don't miss me. Clockwise the cloth.
        The bulb is a blister overhead, the bulb is wet and dripping.

Clock-wise. Cottonmouth, slam-bam, bang up. Bell rung.
        Over the fact of a body. Don't cry.

Later they would say she made it difficult to open the door and
        it took minutes to find scissors able to cut the bedsheet.

Later they would issue a statement that the safety of girls
        in custody is their highest priority.

Paradise Motel

Black flame, blue spoon, now the shadow
draws close a cloak as wide as Lake Michigan,
robed and rocked in god's water, rippling
indigo. From out on the street the rush of cars

weave through lanes their harmonies—
those vessels I've entered one by one,
riding out currents on a raft of fire.
There's an outside and inside to quiet, skin

and pith protecting the body joined lesser
to greater, scintilla to diamond. They said it
wouldn't hurt, and it doesn't. And if the power

takes me, does it matter if they come with salt
water, bring the wheel that turns the breath,
come with help for what can't be helped?

Water in Standing Pools

Not the cry of the owl, lifting off the black
branch on silent wings, not the stranger's face
or the thin blue flame, but flaps and freaks of
moving shadow it's possible to move within,
and moving, make another meaning of the body,
the freight of being a girl for a time released
as wind carries most of the weight across
the field, with some implication of forest
beyond, and the idea you could get there,
somehow, even if it were only a windbreak,
an illusion, but towering, like strangers.
They tell you what to do, and you do it.
Your body accepts them as the ground
accepts rain when it finally falls, the way
you can be, briefly, anything—the virgin
after her child has been despoiled, water
in standing pools before it transubstantiates,
trembling still at each small blow. And
should you believe the only power that holds
is the force the stranger exercises—but, wrong,
not so, you're alone always; and still, your body
bucks beneath the greater, and still, you might
become a remnant of the light that passed over,
a glittering of what once was, a chance.

Winter Shoreline

A single cruiser sawing her way back
to harbor running ahead of those swells
rising like dark planets—then again,

phantoms, they say, live inside the waves
that crash down on our sand,

truths, that before were hidden, slate
green and laced with dirty foam.

Mist and grit and brine. Ocean is also sky.

I walk the between-world, underwater
in open air. Once I saw my mother
there, crouched near the dunes;

her black-draped wings enrobed her
as a judge. The wrack—broken

sticks, crossed bones—strewn
about, as though a forest of ocean
trees had been torn out and tossed up.

The light inside the storm darkened and
silvered them. It was hard to see.

She wore a crimson headscarf and
ministered to a gull, its stove-in
body, its hull ripped open.

A single sandpiper worked the shore.

IV

Sudden Light

If she were a story the wind tells
moving in the leaves,
it would be sudden light. Or broken.
A heron behind chain-link
at the settling ponds.
Glitter of small movements
in the mind, still water. If I could
become moonlight on water,
I might be darkness an eye could
train itself to navigate.
A heron takes to air in the end.
Brokenness is made of breath,
blue wash of twilight, a glimmering
spread of wings, like that evening
my mother flew out of herself
after they shut off the machine, slipped
the last needle, and I whispered,
mom, you're a hero, no one
could have tried harder.

Once

My dad got in the truck and said,
do you want to see me drive
with my knees while I eat breakfast?

No one else was there. He had
a knife and fork, and a plate
of eggs with potatoes which
he wedged onto the steering wheel.

I was kneeling sideways to see better,
and turned to face him. "Yes…" I breathed.
He jammed it in second gear and we rolled
while he ate and steered with his knees.

Happiness threads itself through time.
I still carry it from that day, especially
where the road curved, with houses
perched on one side only and

a steep slope falling away below.

A Field of Energy Knits You to Earth

One explanation could be I've gone fungal
over the years, my filaments
a silver script round your holdfast.
And both of us up for the deal, your sugar
for vital minerals in return. Do you believe
that's the reason I protect you the way I do?
You would be wrong. Silky mycelium
is also a language for silent rootstock.
When a fruiting chantarelle knocks
on the door of the earth, the door opens.
When a tree falls in a far-away forest,
your ears prick up. You know what it's like
to be sawed through; you know what an axe is.
You hear the quiet creaking.
We all live in the gracious shadow
of one mother tree or another.
Just as a mushroom loves night moisture
and morning mist, so too a mushroom
loves mystery. That's how I love you.

Helianthus

Koyu Abe hands out thousands all over Fukushima, drifts
of sunflowers stretching up in abandoned yards

alongside the nuclear plant. Do they really absorb radiation?

You pass a field of sunflowers in Spain, you're on a bus,
I don't know you yet, have you ever been (so) happy:

Endless faces, countless rays. This granary, this cluster-feast:

Van Gogh's painting sunflowers: here's gratitude
and dying every day, here's waiting on the beloved.

Would Gaugin come?   *Let me stay in the compass*

of my heart. And something grants his prayer:
he's already there in blossom and blossom

and blossom. Two million standing in Fukushima.

Hundreds rising at road's edge, an entire field
of bisexual enigma-stars nodding their heads.

Say evanescence. Say inflorescence. You say,

Goddamn, you're pregnant. Goddamn. Wondering or
displeased. Or both. I'm already lobed, tooth-marked,

spiral-flung-out-saffron. We're in the field.

A thousand queens each keeping a secret, a thousand
clandestine florets pollinated by drunkards,

by wade in the water bees up to their knees

in nectar, fetlocks covered with pollen.
The world doesn't need us to know it exists.

At the base of the flower, a door, and a hall

of hidden chambers. To conceal, to save
seeds salted away in the compass of their bed,

chaff for linen, perfect packages packed in a spiral

growth of hair on our baby's head,
I dress her in corduroy and she toddles

toward a giant: long green muscled trunk,

fuzzed and prickled, downward-
gazing head catching light to card and spin,

weave the thread, thrust color back

into the world: *a symphony in blue and yellow.*
What if we're like electrons in two places

at once: up to our knees in nectar, covered

with pollen: why not let joy stick, we
could start over, begin again in flower-speak,

streaming tip of cytoplasm, corolla's open lips,

to smelt, to palp, flush-fleshed   brim
in a flash, come, love that, come slake me.

Invisibility Cloak

Call me purple. Call desire a tangled

skein. Say it lives in every tentacle.

Do you care much for the lonely,

alone in the sea? I've been trying

to plumb the deep. I've been trying

to disappear. Glass squid dive

a thousand meters, light down on

the edge of light. The idea is simple:

we all need chaos and a fellow shade

the same nebulous shape. Which is

to say, I'd like to slide under your cape.

You, with your leaky fiber optics, you

with your smidge of sun, I want to be

the violet that melds into your night.

What Metal Remembers

Yes, I buried a mason jar in that flowerbed
next to our rented cottage, a lock of your hair inside
and a silver ring you rarely wore. What would I give
to climb those stone steps once more, enter the tangle
of violet and cosmos, onyx lips parted, stalks sturdy
enough in this drought for only a single bloom, one
star face with its burning center; what would I give
to kneel and scrabble at our earth with naked fingers?

I could offer all the drowned bells I possess, my cloak
of feathers, my chain-mail, these mother-of-pearl combs
for a chance to touch your black hair again, that lock
darker and younger than we ever were. I would do it.
I want to slip our broken promise onto my hand, how-
ever tarnished, insistent, accustomed to your thicker flesh.
Even after years in darkness among roots weaving and
unweaving their truths, I'm sure metal still remembers you.

The Way It Happened

How many hours
did the sky bear down
before it felt like
a dense fist of pain
loosening?
As though another mouth
stretched an O
inside a body not my own.
A body opened like a split peach,
sleek and rent,
the knees pressed wide.
And was it joy
that lurched downward,
flooding the linoleum?
I rise into the cries.
If blood were silk
and my legs crumbling pillars,
if sound were a long caress
of its own morphology and
screams could plow a room, could
harrow light,
all you would see is red.
Red on the inside of closed lids,
and red the unstoppable force.
Child, listen now,
the evening fills
with blood-colored clouds,
I spend hours falling for your face.
I fall for you like a ripe fruit.
Fallen from the mouth of pleasure.

The Child Who Escaped

I still visit that tree sometimes, though
my daughter's in her thirties, the crook
of the trunk higher these days than any
foolish mother could reach. But back
then I once lifted her into the dusk and
bright of leaves, dappled air silkening
one branch up. Was she more sure
of herself than I thought, or was it
ontological—what new-sprung world
is this canopy-one, to grass, to grow,
to go home to? I tried to change her
mind, cajoled and commanded, but
green's not silent, it speaks its praise
of light and shadow even in slightest
breeze, and a young primate harkens.
Up she scrabbled into small rooms
of luster, lit leaves, green fire, plush
shadow; she climbed into velvet.
She got away from me—this
soul, this agile monkey-creature,
my only one, held in the glittering
world by a greensound song.

Gravid and Amber

When I went into labor at the wrong time, and, finally,
the doctor cut my flesh deep enough
for her to burst from my body, they held her up
and she was blue.

My first thought, how beautiful a color, like Krishna,
the lord of the sky. My next,
if she is Krishna, I won't get to keep her.

They whisked her away, cleared
her airways, returned her. I saw
life and death take each other by the hand.

She was delivered into the light
and that is one fragile truth.
After that, I felt as if there were a space
in my body for death and I needn't worry it.

Here I am now, an older woman, and death
is on my mind, showing up mostly in the slant
of light, its way of falling, gravid and amber.

My father feels it too, this presence
coming in as light; he's humbled by loss, humiliated,
his poor right hand hanging large at the end
of his thinning arm, that relentless heart

hard labor gave him pounding on and on.
One day I say, maybe we can get birds close enough
for you to see them. I'll bring birdseed and
make a warm bed outside, would you like that?

And he answers, yes, please.

What You Are to Me Sleeping

A form of transport. A haunting,
a flight path crossed by insistent owls,
lonely to electric. Your body, a constant.
Next to me. Once I thought I was

a normal high school girl meant to be
heir to an interstellar kingdom. Now,
here I am with you, a human air machine,
you with your prodigal throat. They say

music is a line made of vanishing, I say
a lake where we drift in a boat night after
night, your song elegiac, my hush elegiac.
You nocturne, you soundsurge, ocean me,

crash me, raise me at moonrise. Keep
me in this place I call safe-in-the-world.

How We Learned to Love

This morning's wind is brutal, slapping
the face of my rose. She isn't used to it
and a stipple of bruise breaks out on pink
petals. Rose that I love for all the wrong
reasons, the way you too have loved—
and didn't Mother get after us both, Sister-
of-mine? Because it resembles a camellia
and is called Simplicity, and nothing like
a fist or breast, it puts me in mind of China.
We grew up in the same garden. That's
not simple, either. I love another, too,
a miniature on the left, yellow, bought
from a rosarian at the fair who begged
me to take it. He raised it from a tiny
cutting and thought I was the right one,
even though I warned him, Mister, I got
nothing but shadow. You'll find a place,
he kept saying. I paid him and I did.

Nude Descending a Staircase

Except it's a hallway and no descent involved, no loss of elevation, your warm palette your bright palette swimming toward me. The hanging committee rejected Marcel Duchamp's painting on the grounds that *a nude never descends the stairs, a nude reclines*—and you too would've been rejected by cubists—naked, you're rounded as a nautilus, pink as the lining of a conch, your sex withdrawn into its sheath. In Duchamp's painting, the nude is a mélange of light and dark, a being more piqued as he approaches the edges, the in-betweens, and you are *piqued* too, in the word's meaning of *wounded*. But this morning coming down the hallway, turning into our bedroom, all the shapes organic—sea cucumber, brittle star— nothing cubist at all— yes, today you're free, a natural, a curved and rosy nude stepping down the hallway, and I avert my eyes—my hands two blind men, and you're suddenly the elephant, *very like a wall* says one hand, *very like a rope* says the other, *no*, a hard melon, a bag of kiwis, a smooth stone with the sun inside.

But You Already Know This

Right now, the wind's battering air
around the trees. Don't they look like
little storms at sea? It's hard to keep
loneliness at bay, but we've always kept
tabs on the wind: East, out of the bowl
of night over the Sonora, West, off
the edge of the whirlwind from Alaska.
If it's howling through the vents today,
last week it might've mussed the long hair
of a musk ox. Here in SoCal, dusk goes
creamy, lemon and flour, egg yolk and
butter right through the window, pools
on the shutter. Rain's falling on the North
Coast. Mater, mater, what's the matter?
Mother used to say, Betty Botter bought
a bit of butter, and the dross, the gross,
the dark of matter is bitter, but not more-
so than the higher powers of 'man'. Let's
keep the Archons out of our faces. You've
got a 'bad' attitude that satisfies, and I've
a bitter swagger. If we mix it in our batter
'twill but make you-know-what, Sister.

Sky with Four Suns

Out of flint, a knife,
out of scoring, a line,
mutter of moving water

under sea ice, small waves
threshing small stones.
The ravens arrive at noon.

Light becomes glass,
becomes steel. Dazzles
and wounds. This I accept,

to be held in the way
the sun holds illusion
at 22° distance until

I am emptied out, until
a red-winged blackbird
opens an aperture in sky.

Let the self be woven
in air the blackbirds sail,
in clack and spin of cobbles

as ocean falls together
and apart, self
so tumbled, dislodged,

that you become
the dark blue
that breathes you.

Prayer to Jacaranda

You who hold the knives in light,

bare branches, empty hands lifted,

hear me. I am lost beyond wood.

Body untouched. Begin, I ask you,

with wind, and may doves appear later,

for the body needs, must be, lofted.

Whirlwind or cyclone, unstrung

or restrung. One dark spine with

its dozen fronds. A chest of bone.

Leaf out, Artemis, let chlorophyll

harvest light, let green come to

the beholder; may pleasure come,

so, in me, hungering as a vine, come

twining, turned and turning, let spin

cast its finespun through my interior

trees, violet fire up its flame, burn

as it will beyond lavender to slate.

Forgetting to Eat

It's easy to forget to eat when I'm with my father,
I subsume myself in him, his diet of dust and crumb.
During the Depression, he raised rabbits his older sister
slaughtered. He built the shipping crates while she

skinned the bodies and dressed the meat. He was
younger and allowed to be squeamish. All his life he's
looked away when a syringe fills with red. His blood is low,
he tells me, it barely laps the shore. For this, he sleeps

in his clothes, wrapped in a pull-over, gloves, two throws,
shoes beside the bed waiting like a pair of ancient
geldings still willing to amble the long hall

now that his hunger is for heat, for the warmth
inside of light, the want that carries him out back
to sit full in sun, and almost hear the birds.

Asking the Pears

April. Fierce baby cabbage, spindly tomato,
pears arriving early during this gospel of death
lit like small lanterns, hand-size Neolithic goddesses,
sun-warm, ticking, headless, footless, primordial:
Where will you be when you're gone?

Should I ask the pear cupped in my hand,
filling my palm with its womanly shape?

Pears are inconstant. Never the same.
A drop or two of rosewater, balm
of sunlight in uncertain quantity, ivory flesh—
only sometimes crisp.

Didn't you tell me once their moment
is fragile; watch closely, take them exactly
when rolling their pale gold against the blue,
nymphs fully formed, yes, but still hard?

They refuse a single understanding.
You said I must core, peel, and slice the pears.
Then rub them with lemon juice.

It takes two knives to cut butter into almond flour
to a consistency of coarse meal. You said this.
And I want to say: what becomes of us
afterward? Slow ripples in air. . . . What falls
from the bough rests on the earth. . . .

Snow You Remember

When the wind of your death sweeps through
you go on flying, carried by the blast,
your nomadic soul passing over
our little spit of land.
You hurtle on under the moon
dragging its sack of froth
and spume toward the horizon—
a shade of blue and silver that doesn't exist—
not a lie but a different kind of truth,
an iridescent one.
You work to press on, circumpolar soul
aloft, nothing but the Atlantic
below.
Bird and spirit, you labor over twilight's island
covered with snow you remember,
over oceanic roses—those savage white roses—
in your dress of swansdown.

Late August Garden

Still bold ochre, the yarrow, and heavy

on tilted stems, hollowed out— they're dying
in the usual way,
                           by parts and slowly.
Fistfuls of leaves beneath the oak,
wheat and bleached straw, tawny
                           and umber and dust.
Only the weeds are tantric. Oh, they insist,
                           those rampant ones.

But none of it— my small outpost
                           of wilderness,
bramble and living wall, interior castle—

none of it is exactly true. I am least protected
when alone.
               But, surely, more than withdrawal and
evasion, and a garden built around them. Where am I?

I remember her turning toward me, she
was standing in the doorway
                           of the bedroom,
the light behind her Brazilian pepper tree

with its long delicate fronds, and
the branches shifted in the wind so that
light passed through and among them
                           to enter her room,
and coalesced somehow behind my mother,
                           a wild light
that seemed to hesitate a moment
                           · around her form.

Oh, Marsha, where did our lives go, she exclaimed.
It wasn't long after her diagnosis.
                              Vines sprang up
and clung to my walls,
                    and brambles covered my eyes.

Why is my life over too, I thought, *why must I go with her?*

Velocities

Woman with the salt wind in your mouth,
with a phalanx of gulls on their way to their fortress
in the clouds, you are a far away cirque
of purest agate at ten thousand feet—where
turquoise taught you how to brood into aqua.

When you take small sips of air—
among pear trees, among orange blossoms
and tight apples—light knows your name, Ellen,
it lays down at your verge like a lion.

You've become finally the reverse kiss
of spring, with its velocities and dark
horsemen galloping behind your breastbone.

When you walk the wet sand, fish
celebrate nuptials in the nearest wave
in your name. You understand
how all bright silver things must
pull back into themselves.

Beyond all the chatter, and even
the tears, you are the scar
the plum sews onto its own skin
when sugar splits it open.
You're brimming over.

Our Father Transfigured on His 91ˢᵗ Birthday

Does he hear the flames, the excited way they're gulping air, candles
are voracious; his hand goes out, surely near enough to feel the heat,
our brother pulls the cake back. Just blow, our sister says, and he knows
    only
to lean forward, so she huffs out the flames with her strong lungs and he
    is safe.

Somewhere else, my father bought a hillside lot and built our house,
    working
on weekends. It took him two years. He put by pallets for their wood,
used a claw hammer to extract the nails, and saved the boards
to build our chest of drawers. This we do not remember.

He's alone now on a high mountain where the air is thin, and wind
carries flurries into his eyes. A high mountain where air is thin
can also be called a house. Nothing there but stones and wind
and our father wrapped in a shawl of snow. Beneath the snow
grinds the mountain, its armature, the stone inside the self.

It's Katelyn, grandpa, say good-bye. Our father turns to what he cannot
see—a two-year-old lifted up. The light breaks around her small body,
dazzles his skin, and under his skin. blood threads like red silk.
How *are* you, Katelyn? he croons, Are you *fine*? Can you say *fine*?
This tenderness we do not remember—it must have once fallen on us.

Leviathan

The storm came on sudden leviathan—we'd hardly
commenced struggling with the rigging when
towering over our heads—mountains of water
jade turning pewter, casks sprung, our calves
awash, gale roaring in our faces. *Bad work,*
bad work, cried Simon, holding by a shroud,
the sea will have her way! And still our master
slept in starboard quadrant as the ship heaved
over precipice and slid into wallow, rollers
like sheaves foaming on the windward side,
mast bare-poled, cross-hatched, torn of her canvas.
We worked like phantoms, our lives' forfeit,
unlashing cordage, bailing the hull while *he*
dreamed on oblivious. Matthew, stricken with
anger as much as fear, roared into a lull, *Does his*
magnitude diminish? Then must we perish all!
and every soul on deck heard, yet still *he* did not
stir. I tell you the world upended, sea black
as blood and hard what should be soft, sky as
much water as air, our mouths white slits. James
finally knelt, *Sir, we flounder,* lips close to the shell
of his ear, even then we dared not touch him.

Eye of the Deer

Suckling pigs the size of infants,
their skin golden and glistening
with fat, hanging from hooks
in the windows of pocket
eateries on the narrow streets
of Toledo—we saw them after-
wards, those lechones—little
ones voracious for milk, guzzlers,
eager milkers, hungry mouths.

The woman I was with believed
St John of the Cross betrayed himself
with rapture, the language of lover and
beloved, too much, too sexual—later
she would shave her head and become
a Buddhist nun—but that day we made
our clumsy, in-the-moment translations
on the train to one another as though
searching through those songs of longing

for what we would not understand
and everywhere the most audacious
intimacies, reading them aloud,
eyes on each other, and would she
taste the tenderness of new life, let
the grease smear her lips? She would not.
Hills the color of flayed leather,
rounding their curves, a view of Toledo,
the holy city like a silver brooch

against the breast of storm—El Greco
painted it that way. Landscape painting
forbidden since the Council of Trent. He
did it anyway, a rugged promontory
clothed in green, claiming color as
the most ungovernable element.
How could that be in La Mancha—

small spears and knives of grass as fresh
with desire as flesh and vein, flush with

dark water? Only if landscape is
encounter, not description, if the eye
says what it does not see, the steep
where the deer grazes, unquestioning
sourceless light. My body as escarpment,
slope, rockfall, as thin soil tunneled by
new grass. Under a dome of storm.
The eye of the deer also eye of
the lover. What is it You want of me?

Pelican Entangled in Kelp

When flight faltered, he dipped lower
and the wind would not lift him and
wings couldn't carry him, slender bones
not strong enough, the pelican

plummeted into the ocean which used to be
home, used to be an element that nurtured
but oil on wings let in cold, no longer
watertight, no longer able to dive or swim,

now he sank, struggled up for air
and water filled his lungs, this fluid
that buoyed him all the other days
of his life, this water took his breath,

and the blood, sluggish, staggered;

and when the heart couldn't pump,
when the heart without air, spasmed,
when the heart convulsed,
the eyes no longer saw—

the mind saw the last green and gold,
the bronze of the kelp lifting from
her holdfast, long limbs wrapping him,
surrounding him, shrouding him

and her fan-like leaves drifted, and
the arrows of her seed let go, and
the fruit of her sex lifted, and copper
ropes held him as in a hammock,

and in this way, the moon, urging
wave onto wave, rocked the dying
to shore where their great bodies,
stranded now, came to rest.

Notes

"Horses Resting" is based on a photo from the Edson Smith Vintage Photo Collection at the Santa Barbara Art Museum. The poem is for Enid Osborn and horses she has known.

"What It Sounded Like on the Way to Calvary" is based on a painting by Bruegel in which the setting depicted is not Palestine but sixteenth-century Flanders.

"A History of Lament" addresses the story of Cain and Abel and is dedicated to mothers who lose children to violence.

"The Afterlife of Flames" refers to the rare California fire poppy, which grows after a major burn. Its seeds can lie dormant for decades. They bloom only for a day.

"American Megafauna" refers to the hope of the "founding fathers" that proof of the existence of large mammals might be found on the North American continent. Thomas Jefferson called the first discovered mammoth fossil "our incognitum."

"Indelible" is based on the phrase "Indelible in the hippocampus is the laughter . . . ," which Dr. Christine Blasey Ford used to describe the memory of her assault. The opening sonnet is after Terrance Hayes.

"The Boy Who Went Looking" is based on a nineteenth-century photo of an indigenous child from the Edson Smith Vintage Photo Collection at the Santa Barbara Art Museum.

"Girls in Custody" is dedicated to Rosemary Summers who died in the custody of the Juvenile Justice system.

"Paradise Motel" was written to address the opioid epidemic and in response to a painting by Patricia Chidlaw of an older motel on Sunset Boulevard.

"Water in Standing Pools" takes some of its inspiration and language from "Frost at Midnight" by Coleridge.

"Helianthus" is a reference to the sunflowers planted after the Fukushima nuclear disaster, and is dedicated to Jorge de la O.

"Invisibility Cloak" refers to glass squid, which can instantly change color and shape to hide themselves, and prefer to reside at extreme depths.

"Sky with Four Suns" is in response to composer John Luther Adams' piece called *Canticles of the Sky*. One of the movements is entitled "Sky with Four Suns."

"Leviathan" is a response to the painting by Delacroix, *Christ in the Storm on the Sea of Galilee*.

"Pelican Entangled in Kelp" is an ekphrastic poem, based on Lynn Hanson's painting entitled *Shroud*.

Acknowledgments

Grateful acknowledgment is made to the editors of the following publications in which some of these poems previously appeared, sometimes in slightly different form:

Big Enough for Words: Poems and Vintage Photographs from California's Central Coast (Gunpowder Press, 2021), edited by David Starkey, Chryss Yost, and George Yatchisin: "Horses Resting" and "The Boy Who Went Looking"; *Interlitq*: "The Way It Happened"; *Miramar*: "The Seer and the Seen"; *Negative Capability Press*: "Velocities" and "What Metal Remembers"; *North American Review*: "Origin" and "The Day I Was Protected"; *Pandemic Puzzles* (Blue Light Press, 2021), edited by Diane Frank and Prartho Sereno: "A History of Lament"; *Pedestal*: "Crevasse," "A History of Lament," and "What It Sounded Like on the Way to Calvary"; *Poetry Pacific*: "Invisibility Cloak" and "The Afterlife of Flames"; *Prairie Schooner*: "Paradise Motel"; *Pratnik*: "Girls in Custody" and "Helianthus"; *Salt*: "Late August Garden," "Eye of the Deer," and "Forgetting to Eat"; *Solo*: "Snow You Remember"; *Terminus*: "American Megafauna."

This collection is born from the love and support of California's Central Coast poetry communities—Sunday Poets, Summer Women, Poetry Liberation Front, and the Salonistas. You know who you are. Thank you for your essential help in shaping these poems. They could not have come into form without you. Special gratitude to Joyce Jenkins, Christopher Buckley, and Laure-Anne Bosselaar for the never-ending encouragement. I am incredibly grateful to the editors of the Pitt Poetry Series for selecting the manuscript and working with me to make it a better book. Thank you for your guidance. To my brothers and, especially, my sisters, Janet and Nancy, we share the best laughs and always have. To our parents, Donald and Shirley, you gave us life and shaped our being, and supported us through all the travail, you are the pulsars in our firmament. To Nereyda de la O, giving birth and bringing you up has been the greatest honor of my life. You, Henry, and Caleaf are hope pressing against the future. Love to Phil Taggart—I am your creature.